THE LONDONDERRY ALBUM

Portraits from a Great House in the 1890s

Introduced by The Marquess of Londonderry

Mary Harvey

BLOND & BRIGGS

First published 1978 by Blond & Briggs Ltd, London, and Tiptree,
Colchester, Essex © Copyright 1978 the Marquess of Londonderry
SBN 85634 098 7

Previous page: Contenders in the paternity stakes.
Above: Theresa and Reginald.
Below: Reginald Helmsley, Lord Londonderry and the Prince
of Wales.

The first account of the Wynyard darkroom appeared two years
ago in an evocative article by Brian Masters in *Vogue*. The en-
thusiasm of Beatrix Miller, the editor of *Vogue*, and the praise for
Reginald's skill from David Bailey spurred me to undertake further
research on my own and to bring the darkroom and its contents
to a wider audience. My thanks to them, and to Hal Bethell,
manager of BBC Radio Cleveland, who first broadcast the story of
the darkroom. As a result of the broadcast, I was approached by
Henry Middleton, the director of the Gray Art Gallery in Hartlepool, who arranged the first public exhibition in December 1977
of the photographs and the contents of the darkroom. This in turn
gave rise to another exhibition at the Bowes Museum at Barnard
Castle in July 1978. I am especially grateful to Roy Round, who
made the first prints after the discovery of the darkroom, and to
Dennis Wompra who, with his staff, shouldered the burden of
producing the prints for the exhibitions and for publication.

To Frederick and Reginald

*To Tom and Mary
with many thanks for all
their hospitality and kindness
during our nostalgic return
to Norfolk in 1982
love from us all
Alastair*

INTRODUCTION

by
The Marquess of Londonderry

It may seem strange that one can live in a house, however large, for nearly thirty years and be unaware of the existence of a treasure trove. Yet this is what happened to me at Wynyard, my family's ancestral home in County Durham. No one had ever mentioned the existence of a perfectly preserved Victorian darkroom and it was only by chance that I came to hear of it.

Having always had an interest in photography it had long been my intention to make a darkroom of my own at Wynyard and I happened one day to ask Ernie Stephenson, the odd-job man who had worked there for some thirty years, if he could suggest somewhere. He replied that there already was a darkroom, but there was nothing of any value therein. This turned out to be a masterpiece of understatement, for on unlocking the door I discovered a Victorian darkroom in its pristine state. Everything was exactly where it had been left when the last person to use the darkroom had locked the door some fifty years ago. What struck me immediately was the marvellous quality of the Victorian photographer's equipment. The porcelain sink and the beautifully made photographer's bench naturally occupied pride of place against one of the dark purple walls, while next to them was a complete Magic Lantern outfit, seemingly undamaged. On the bench and the shelves, scattered in profusion, were porcelain trays, half empty bottles of photographic chemicals in all shapes and sizes, boxes of printing paper, in fact all the wherewithal of the photographer's art. A greater contrast to the plastic efficiency of the modern darkroom could not be imagined. The real treasures, such as the early folding and box cameras and some glass negatives, were hidden in several large wooden chests. How could I have been unaware of this treasure, I asked myself. The darkroom was halfway down a rickety old staircase which leads from the old guest wing to the statue gallery on the ground floor. The staircase could only have been used by the domestic staff, since the only room it leads to is an old store room. I had of course been aware of this staircase, access to which was through a door in the corridor known as the Duke's Gallery, the old guest wing of the house named after the Duke of Wellington, but I had always avoided it because the staircase also led to the dome high above the statue gallery and, like most sufferers from vertigo, heights held a horrible fascination for me. Furthermore there was the problem of keys which were always being lost or mislaid and never replaced.

My excitement at the discovery was only equalled by my curiosity to find out the identity of the photographer. A leather camera case stamped with a coronet and the initials T.L. was the first obvious clue. These initials could only refer to Theresa Londonderry, wife of the 6th Marquess, a great beauty and well-known political hostess. Other clues were a pair of small black crutches in the corner of the darkroom, a box containing a piece of mineral stone and bearing the name Lord Reginald Stewart and most significantly a letter dated May 23, 1898 addressed to Lord Reginald Stewart. The letter dealt with geological matters and ended with the sentence, 'I hope you have returned completely recovered from the illness you have been suffering from.' Even before the plates had been developed, this was more than sufficient evidence for me to speculate on the identity of the photographer.

Reginald Stewart was the younger son of the 6th Marquess of Londonderry. All I knew of his existence was what I had heard from my father who also told me he was a love child, Theresa's offspring from an extra-marital adventure. A very gifted boy with a marked scientific bent, his talents only briefly found their expression, since he departed this life at the age of nineteen, a victim of the then incurable scourge of tuberculosis. All I knew of Theresa was that she was a famous political hostess and that her nickname in later life was Guy. That she and her son Reginald were gifted photographers I had never heard from any members of the family and I must confess I found it hard to think of the great hostess Theresa dirtying her hands with all the messy photographic chemicals, but apparently she was not alone among aristocratic ladies in trying her hand at photography. It is frustrating indeed to reflect that had I known of the darkroom's existence some twenty years ago, I could have had answers to all my questions from my grandmother, who married Reginald's half-brother Charles, and from Lady Helen Ilchester who was Reginald's half-sister and who appears in many of the photographs. It is also strange that my father never mentioned the darkroom to me, since photographs of him as a child and as a young man are among the collection. My task therefore of identifying the photographers has not been an easy one and I have had to rely very largely on circumstantial evidence. Obviously no more photographs were taken by Reginald after 1899, the year of his death, and Theresa's photographic activities ended in 1915 when her husband died and she had to leave Wynyard.

The factual proof that Theresa and Reginald took most of the photographs came from a letter I received from an old lady who wrote to me after the first exhibition of the photographs in Hartlepool last year. The old lady was the late Mrs Elsie Apperley, the widow of a contemporary of Reginald and the daughter-in-law of N. W. Apperley who was private secretary to Theresa's husband and son of the famous sporting writer of the nineteenth century, Nimrod. Mrs Apperley told me many interesting things concerning Reginald's paternity, but that would be anticipating another stage in the story which ought to unfurl chronologically. It is thanks to Mrs Apperley incidentally that I was able to identify many of the sitters in the photographs. If she had not written to me, I would not have seen her family's marvellous photograph albums which were the Rosetta stone that enabled me to unravel most of the mysteries of the darkroom.

Theresa was born in 1865, the oldest daughter of the 19th Earl of Shrewsbury, the Premier Earl of England. In 1875 she married Charles, Viscount Castlereagh, son and heir of the 5th Marquess of Londonderry, her senior by four years. Castlereagh's best man was Reginald, Viscount Helmsley, son of the first Earl of Feversham, who the following year married Theresa's sister, Lady Muriel Chetwynd-Talbot. After their marriage the Castlereaghs went to live at Kirkby Hall near Bedale in Yorkshire which was not very far from Ainderby where the Helmsleys lived. Such propinquity and the choice of Helmsley as best man were to have fateful results. After the birth of her daughter Helen in 1876 and her son Charles in 1878 Theresa gave birth to a second son, Reginald, in December 1879. Exactly who Reginald's father was, no one can say for sure, but everyone at the time was agreed that it was certainly not Theresa's husband. This is what my father told me, although he did not elaborate. The most likely contender in the paternity stakes was Theresa's brother-in-law, the aforementioned Reginald Helmsley, one of the best looking men of his generation. Undoubtedly Theresa had been having an affair with Helmsley, for it was the talk of London. In his memoirs Chips Channon relates how my grandmother, Edith Londonderry, told him that it was this affair which Lady de Grey, Theresa's arch rival in society and amorous intrigues, had brought to the notice of Lord Castlereagh, in a fit of jealous rage over Theresa's fling with Lord Annaly. It was this affair incidentally, not the one with Harry Cust which Anita Leslie mentions in her book *Edwardians in Love*, that impaired Theresa's marriage, although it did not bring about a silence between them of thirty years' duration. This wild exaggeration, based purely on hearsay, is disproved by the esteem in which Theresa is known to have been held by her husband, an esteem which was mutual. The photograph of Theresa and her husband holding my father and his sister Maureen, their grandchildren, on their knees is not that of a husband and wife who have not talked to each other for nearly thirty years. There is no evidence either that Theresa's affair with Helmsley caused any estrangement between her and her sister. Undoubtedly any husband who is cuckolded by his best man is bound to react fairly strongly, particularly if there is a child from the liaison. Reginald was, however, acknowledged as one of the family and given the family name. He himself probably never knew the story behind his paternity.

The issue of Reginald's paternity was not quite so simple as I had imagined. At the time of his birth it was assumed that Helmsley was the father and subsequent generations were always told this story, but the late Elsie Apperley who contacted me after the Hartlepool exhibition insisted that Reginald's father was Edward VII. Furthermore she told me that Reginald was known as Rex and that the boy's supposedly congenital lameness was the result of being pushed off Theresa's lap as a baby by her husband who had been overcome by jealousy. Reginald, derived as it is from the Latin *rex*, was the name Theresa gave the child to spite her husband. Far-fetched it might all appear, but would Theresa have been so insensitive as to call her love child by the name of her lover? Mrs Apperley's version cannot be dismissed out of hand because the source is impeccable: her father-in-law N. W. Apperley was the private secretary of Theresa's husband and without doubt privy to all the family secrets. As none of Reginald's contemporaries are alive, it is impossible to verify the story. I have never heard this story from any member of the family, even though I recently met an Irish lady who told me she had heard it from her mother. The trouble was that so many paternities were attributed to Edward that it was inevitable for rumours to abound. It is quite possible that Theresa had a fling with Edward, for many high-born ladies did at one time or another. The photograph of Helmsley does not provide positive proof of paternity, although if one looks hard enough one might detect a slight resemblance. It will have to be left therefore as a matter for fascinating conjecture. I myself am inclined to accept that the father was Helmsley, but I do believe that part of Mrs Apperley's story which concerns the laming incident.

Of Reginald himself we do not know a great deal. The photographs show he was a handsome boy and from all accounts he was also very intelligent. My father had heard nothing but good of him. His delicate health ruled out a conventional education in schools and he was therefore educated at home by tutors. The circumstances of his birth and his frail hold on life probably made Theresa's relationship with her son an extremely close one and their mutual passion for photography is indicative of this. The idea that Theresa could ever have been unkind to him – a rumour based on pure hearsay – is too preposterous to entertain for a moment. Reginald spent most of his life at the two Londonderry properties in the North of England, Wynyard Park and Seaham Hall. The photographs show that he also spent some time at Mountstewart too, but undoubtedly he preferred to be in the North of England. At Seaham he could indulge his passion for trains and he was able to drive the locomotive engine many times from Seaham to Sunderland.

The Londonderry Railway was the creation of the 3rd Marquess of Londonderry, Charles Stewart, an energetic and courageous soldier who together with his remarkable wife, Frances Anne, an intimate friend of Disraeli, made the Londonderry family business one of the great entrepreneurial concerns of the North-East. Seaham Harbour's importance as a coal-mining port was entirely due to the determination of Charles and his wife who had developed the town as a rival to neighbouring Sunderland. Eventually Sunderland was to eclipse the smaller port and Londonderry Railway was taken over by the North-Eastern in 1900.

Reginald's ill-health did not entirely prevent him from leading a normal life, even if he could not go to school like his half-brother, Charles. He appears in the enchanting photograph of the bicyclists which was taken shortly before he died. Thereafter he appeared in only two of the photographs, both of which show unmistakable signs of his illness and his lameness. The disease was to progress with frightening rapidity. In all probability it was also tuberculosis which killed Reginald's putative father Helmsley who died in Madeira, in 1881 at the age of twenty-nine. From all accounts Reginald bore his lot with great stoicism and always retained his good nature. This is certainly borne out by the few photographs taken of him in the final years, particularly the pathetic picture of him wrapped in a rug. He was sent to the warmer climes of Tenerife and South Africa in a desperate effort to regain his health, but to no avail. In South Africa he spent some time at the Kimberley sanatorium and also with Cecil Rhodes who esteemed him highly. In a letter to her mother dated April 4, 1889, Lady Helen Stewart writes, 'I must confess I feel very unhappy at what you say about Reggie's cough: it must be very bad and how wretched he will be when you leave him. Don't you think someone ought to be with him, as of course he will feel the loneliness after having had you.' One has a heartrending picture of poor little Reggie coughing his life away and perhaps with more than an inkling that he was about to die. On September 8, Theresa wrote to Cecil Rhodes, 'You will, I know, be sorry to hear that Reggie is very weak – he is really too good for this world, his patience is exemplary.' His condition steadily deteriorated, his voice becoming almost inaudible according to his half-brother Charles who had to postpone his wedding because of Reginald's grave condition. On Monday morning October 9, 1899, shortly after seven o'clock, death brought a merciful release from Reginald's terrible suffering. His mother Theresa, his grandmother Lady Shrewsbury and his half-sister Helen were present at his deathbed. Having spent so much of his brief life in Seaham Reginald had expressed a wish to be buried there and this was duly done. The funeral took place at St Mary's Church in Old Seaham on Thursday, October 12. The town showed its respect by closing the shops for two hours. Reginald Helmsley,

Reginald Stewart's half-brother, was present at the funeral and N. W. Apperley, father-in-law of the late Elsie Apperley, was one of the pall bearers. A beautiful Celtic cross surmounts his grave in the neglected cemetery of the church.

The photographs have at last received the praise which is their due and this book is the ultimate posthumous tribute to a remarkable young man and his no less talented mother. The quality of the photographs has already been praised by one more fitted than me, the photographer David Bailey, who has compared Reginald to Lartigue, the great French photographer. The comparison with Lartigue is high praise indeed as well as being apt, for both Reginald and Lartigue came from aristocratic backgrounds and both practised photography as a hobby. Lartigue however was lucky enough to be born with good health and has been acknowledged as one of the most remarkable photographers in the history of the art.

The photographs are single portraits, small and large groups, and some memorable landscape studies. The group photographs give a picture of life in a great country house at the turn of the century, recording the visits of famous politicians and the constant house parties. It is said that the statesman A. J. Balfour, a frequent visitor, detested having his photograph taken, but one has the feeling he was delighted to oblige Reginald and his mother. Unlike most group photographs of the period, the sitters rarely have that resigned patient look on their faces and one suspects that both photographers knew exactly when to release the shutter. The settings for the photographs, usually on the steps of the south terrace at Wynyard or in the conservatory, were chosen with much care and show the smaller groups to great advantage. These photographs, together with those of Lord Castlereagh and his sister Helen, are some of the most beautiful and evocative in the collection. What is especially noticeable about these photographs is the understanding of light, which is of course the key to the mastery of photography. As Bailey says, 'Photography at the time Reginald was taking pictures depended much more on the feel of the thing. By this I mean one had to feel the amount of light there was to make an exposure with no help from today's sophisticated exposure meters.'

The mere fact of their discovery in a perfectly preserved Victorian darkroom has conferred upon the photographs a unique interest, but as a collection they have an obvious artistic value and are also of historical significance. The photographs of Salisbury and Balfour on their frequent visits to the various residences of the Londonderry family are interesting, since more often than not they are shown in informal poses. The fascinating picture of Lord Salisbury with the Chinese dignitaries is a puzzle, since there is no clue as to where it was taken. It is certainly not at any Londonderry property, but it could have been taken at Hatfield or even on the bridge over the Serpentine. Presumably it was given by Lord Salisbury to the 6th Marquess. Of particular historical importance is the photograph of the Privy Council meeting held at Wynyard in 1903, the first occasion on which a Council had been held in a country house belonging to a subject since October 1625, when Charles I held one at Wilton, the house of the then Lord Chamberlain, Lord Pembroke. This photograph is additionally interesting, for it records the only occasion on which King Edward brought his favourite mistress Mrs Keppel to Wynyard. The early photographs of Frances Anne and those of the 5th Marquess with his family are fascinating, for it is always interesting to see photographs of people whose painted likenesses have been a part of one's life. Lastly one must mention the photograph of the German governess Fräulein Sturmfels with the broomstick in the Italian garden. This extraordinary study has a timeless quality which warrants its inclusion in any collection of remarkable photographs.

Although neither Reginald nor his mother were the only people to use the darkroom there is no denying that it is his spirit which pervades it. The crutches in the corner, the wooden box bearing his name, the piece of mineral stone, the letter, all these signs indicate that the darkroom was his domain. It is difficult to conjecture what his life might have been had he lived. He could have become another Lartigue, but it is possible that contemporary conventions might have prevented him from developing his gift to the full. One therefore trusts that this book will ensure him an honourable place in the ranks of those who have enhanced the art of photography. I am glad to think that I have played some part in this posthumous tribute to the memory of a brave and talented young man who departed this life all too soon. Let a Seaham Harbour man, Mr G. Halliwell, who had known Reginald from his boyhood, have the final word. In a letter to the *Daily Chronicle* on October 13, 1899, he says, 'I always held the idea that if Nature had provided a healthy and robust body for his soul to live in, he would have had a brilliant future before him.'

Frances Anne, wife of the 3rd Marquess. A remarkable businesswoman, an excellent writer, a hostess on a grand scale and a much-admired friend of Disraeli: a truly formidable woman of her time.
Photograph taken in Llandudno shortly before she died in 1865.

Lord Herbert Vane Tempest and his sister Aline astride one of the lions on the Lion Bridge at Wynyard. Herbert was the second son of the 5th Marquess and Aline the only daughter, who later married Lord Allendale.
Photograph taken in the early 1860s.

Lady Aline Vane Tempest 'waiting for the train'.
Photograph taken in the early 1860s.

Henry, 5th Marquess.
Photograph taken in the early 1860s.

Charles, Viscount Seaham, later 6th Marquess.
Photograph taken in the early 1860s.

Theresa, wife of the 6th Marquess and mother of Reginald, who took this photograph in the conservatory at Wynyard *c*1890. Theresa was the daughter of the Earl of Shrewsbury. A noted beauty and prominent society hostess, she had several affairs during her marriage. Despite her flightiness, Theresa's husband was well aware of his wife's remarkable qualities and respected her for them. She for her part was devoted to him and was heartbroken when he died.

Right

Charles Stewart, 6th Marquess, husband of Theresa, and father of the 7th Marquess and Lady Helen Stewart. A prominent member of Edwardian society, he was also a political figure of some importance, although not over-endowed with ability. Among the positions he held were Lord Lieutenant of Ireland (1886–1889), President of the Board of Education (1902) – an appointment which owed more to his friendship with the King, Londonderry's enemies maintained, than to any aptitude for the post – and he was made Privy Councillor in 1903. This last was conferred at a special, if not unique, meeting of the Privy Council held at Wynyard at the insistence of Edward VII. This was the only time the King brought with him his favourite mistress, Mrs Keppel, to Wynyard.

Lady Helen Stewart, daughter of the 6th Marquess, with 'Vicky' at Wynyard in 1890. Photograph by Reginald or Theresa.

Lady Helen in fancy dress, taken at Mountstewart *c*1890 by Reginald or Theresa.

Charles, Viscount Castlereagh. Later, as 7th Marquess, he became a passionate aviator who continued to fly his own aircraft until shortly before he died. He was Minister of Aviation in the National Government of 1931 until his cavalier dismissal by Baldwin.

Photographed at Wynyard c1890 by his mother, Theresa or his half-brother Reginald.

Charles, Lord Castlereagh, in uniform.
Photograph by Reginald or Theresa c1890.

Charles, 'the good shot'.
Photographed at Wynyard *c*1890 by Reginald or Theresa.

Reginald Stewart, son of Theresa. His father was probably Reginald Helmsley, son of the first Earl of Feversham, brother-in-law to Theresa and best man to her husband. Reginald was born in 1789, almost a year after his half-brother Charles. It was always assumed that Helmsley was the father; but, according to the late Elsie Apperley, wife of a close friend of Reginald's and daughter-in-law of the private secretary of the 6th Marquess, the real father was Edward VII.

Lord Reginald recuperating from one of his many bouts of illness.
Photograph by Theresa at Mountstewart in the early 1890s.

Lord Reginald photographed by Theresa at Wynyard c1890.

Charles, Lord Castlereagh and his sister Lady Helen Stewart in fancy dress.
Taken by Reginald or Theresa in the 1890s, in the conservatory at Wynyard.

Charles, Helen and Reginald, with 'Lina', taken by Theresa
c1890.

Charles, Helen and Reginald in sporting garb, taken by
Theresa *c*1890.

Robin Stewart, later 8th Marquess, taken by Theresa at Wynyard *c*1908. Before he succeeded, he became MP for South Down. A perceptive journalist and writer, he interviewed both Hitler and Goebbels and, later, was the only coal-owner's son to advocate nationalization of the mines.

Lady Maureen Stewart, who later married Oliver Stanley, the Conservative politician, and Robin, later 8th Marquess, sitting on the knees of their grandparents, the 6th Marquess and Marchioness of Londonderry.

Right
Lady Maureen and Lord Robin with their mother Edith, wife of the 7th Marquess. She was a great hostess in the Londonderry tradition, a writer, and an intimate friend of Ramsay Macdonald. Photograph by Theresa.

Grandmother, mother and daughter. The Countess of Shrewsbury (mother of Theresa), Lady Helen Stewart and Theresa, wife of the 6th Marquess.

Charles and Reginald sparring with a friend or cousin.
Photograph by Theresa c1890.

Helen, Reginald, Charles and a friend on the lake at Wynyard.
Taken by Theresa *c*1890.

Left to right: Sir William Eden (father of Sir Anthony), the 6th Marquess, Lady Melgund, Lady Helen Stewart and Lord Castlereagh. Photograph by Reginald or Theresa at Wynyard in September 1890.

Back row, left to right: Mr Eminson, the 6th Marquess, N. W. Apperley (private secretary to Lord Londonderry). *Front row*: Mrs Eminson, Lady Helen Stewart, Fräulein Sturmfels (German governess). *Seated on floor*: Lord Castlereagh. Taken in conservatory at Wynyard by Reginald or Theresa in August 1891.

The 6th Marquess (2nd from left) sitting next to A. J. Balfour.
Taken outside the conservatory at Wynyard by Reginald or
Theresa *c*1890.

Lady Shrewsbury, mother of Theresa, seated in front of trap.
Taken in front of Wynyard by Reginald or Theresa c1890.

Posed photograph of a frequent house-guest, taken by Reginald or Theresa in the conservatory at Wynyard *c*1890.

Lord Henry Vane Tempest photographed outside Mountstewart *c*1890, by Reginald or Theresa.

Fräulein Sturmfels, the German governess, taken in the
pleasure gardens at Wynyard *c*1890 by Reginald or Theresa.

The front of Mountstewart. Taken by Reginald or Theresa
c1890.

The old school at Wynyard. Taken by Reginald or Theresa
*c*1890.

View of the dairy at Wynyard, whose portico it modestly resembles. Taken by Reginald or Theresa *c* 1890.

Right: Mary Cornelia, her husband the 5th Marquess, the Prince of Wales and his wife Alexandra. Taken at Wynyard in the early 1880s. Photographer unknown.

Group photographed outside the entrance to Mountstewart. The 5th Marquess is on the extreme left, Lord Randolph Churchill on the left inside the doorway, and Mary Cornelia, wife of the 5th Marquess, leaning against the wall on the right. Jenny Churchill is seated in the middle of the front row. Photograph taken in the early 1880s.

A visit to England by emissaries from the emperor of China in the 1890s, showing Lord Salisbury (4th from left) the then Prime Minister and Curzon, the Foreign Secretary.

Bicycling was the rage in the 90s: this group shows – (from left) Lord Castlereagh, Fräulein Sturmfels, Lady Helen in the centre, her father next to her, Reginald, and Mr Apperley the private secretary. Taken by Theresa 1892–3.

Back row: Lady Helen Stewart, Lord Castlereagh (centre), and Reginald (first on the right). Lady Shrewsbury is seated on the right.
Taken by Theresa in the early 1890s.

Group of children: Reginald in the back row (left), Lady
Helen seated centre. Taken by Theresa *c*1890.

Horse-drawn carriage outside the entrance of Wynyard. Lady
Helen is seated in the carriage and her father is standing on the
right of the group.

Horse-drawn group including Lady Helen (holding whip) and
the German governess in the middle.
Taken by Reginald or Theresa.

Sparring group posed with the 6th Marquess as referee in the
middle. The contestant on the left is the Hon. Harry White.
Photograph by Reginald c1890.

The head gardener's house at Wynyard in the 1890s. The kitchen garden, into whose wall the house is built, still functions.

A group of worthies employed at Wynyard, dressed in their
Sunday best.
Photographed by Reginald *c*1880.

A group of the staff seated at the foot of the steps outside Lady
Londonderry's bedroom.
Photograph by Reginald or Theresa *c*1890.

Gardener at Wynyard posed by Reginald c1890.

Falconer taken at Wynyard by Reginald or Theresa in the
1890s.

Not the laundry but the dairy, showing dairy-maids churning
butter. Theresa and Lady Helen are in the group under the
window.
Photographed at Wynyard by Reginald c1890.

The head gardener's house at Wynyard at the turn of the century. Photograph by Theresa.

A machine for determining or adjusting the gauge of railway lines, photographed on the stretch of line between Seaham and Sunderland. Taken by Reginald, who was a railway enthusiast.

Group on the Seaham/Sunderland railway line.
Photograph by Reginald c1890.

Group outside a mine in Seaham. The 8th Marquess is second
from left.

Another group outside a mine in Seaham, taken during the First World War. *Left*: Malcolm Dillon, manager of the Londonderry collieries; *2nd from right*: Theresa; *3rd from right*: her grandson the 8th Marquess and next to him his mother Edith, wife of the 7th Marquess.

Group taken at the time of Lord Salisbury's visit to Belfast in 1893, in the grounds of Mountstewart.

Back row: 6th Marquess (5th from left), Edward Carson, famous barrister and leading Unionist (7th from left).

Front row: Lord Bishop of Derry (2nd from left), Theresa Lady Londonderry (4th from left), Lord Salisbury on her left and next to him his daughter Lady Gwendoline Cecil.

The unique meeting of the Privy Council held at Wynyard on October 19, 1903. In his memoirs Sir Almeric Fitzroy, the then Clerk to the Privy Council, says that 'the last occasion on which a Council had been held in a country house belonging to a subject was in October 1625 when Charles II held one at Wilton, the Lord Pembroke of the day being his Chamberlain.

Lady Londonderry was greatly excited over the event and was particularly pleased to learn that the King desired the documents connected with the Council to be headed "at the Court at Wynyard", which is indeed the old style.'

The King also brought with him his mistress Mrs Keppel on this occasion. She is on the extreme left in the front row.

Back row: 6th Marquess (2nd from left), Henry Chaplin (4th from left), Lord Henry Vane Tempest (5th from left), Adolphus Vane Tempest (2nd from right). *Front row*: Lord Herbert Vane Tempest (left), Lord Ormonde (3rd from left), Hon. James Lowther (4th from left).

Back row: Christopher Sykes (2nd from left), Lord Ormonde (4th from left), Hon. James Lowther (4th from right), Henry Chaplin (3rd from right).

Middle: Prince of Wales (2nd from left).

Front, seated on ground: Marquis de Soveral, Lady Helen Stewart, 6th Marquess, N. W. Apperley.

A shooting party at Wynyard. The Marquis de Soveral was a well-known figure in society, known for his volubility, he was nicknamed 'the Blue Monkey'. Christopher Sykes was an intimate of the King, idolizing him to such an extent that he nearly bankrupted himself entertaining 'Tum-Tum'.

Back row: Lord Herbert Vane Tempest (2nd from left), Cecil Rhodes, Lord Castlereagh, Lord Henry Vane Tempest (5th from right).
Front row: Reginald Stewart (left), Lady Helen Stewart (4th from left), 6th Marquess (4th from right), Fräulein Sturmfels (2nd from right).

Back row: Lady Coke (4th from left), Hon. James Lowther (next to her), Lord Coke (6th from left), Duke of Montrose (slightly behind Coke), Princess of Wales (6th from right), Lord Herbert Vane Tempest, Henry Chaplin, Count Herbert Bismarck, N. W. Apperley (2nd from right).

Middle row, seated: Prince of Wales (centre), Duchess of Montrose (next to him), Lady Randolph Churchill (2nd from right). *Front row*: M. de Falbe, 6th Marquess, Lord Randolph Churchill.

Visit by the Prince and Princess of Wales to Plas Machynlleth, the Londonderry house in Wales.

Back row: Christopher Sykes (2nd from left), Lady Aline Beaumont (4th from left), 6th Marquess, Lord Henry Vane Tempest, the Prince of Wales, Lord Herbert Vane Tempest, (3rd from right), N. W. Apperley (extreme right).

Front row: Mary Cornelia, Dowager Marchioness (3rd from left), the Princess of Wales (centre).

Another royal visit to Wynyard, photographed by Reginald in 1890.
Back row: Christopher Sykes (3rd from left), the Princess of Wales (6th from left), 6th Marquess (next to her), Lady Helen Stewart, Prince of Wales, Lord Ormonde (3rd from right), N. W. Apperley (extreme right).
Front row: Theresa (5th from left), Henry ('Squire') Chaplin (3rd from right).

Informal group during a house-party at Wynyard. The 6th
Marquess is on the extreme left of the front row and A. J.
Balfour, with tennis racquet, on extreme right. The Hon.
Harry White on his right. Photograph by Reginald or Theresa.

Small group photographed by Theresa c1890.   *Centre*: Lord Reginald Stewart (2nd from left).
Back row: Lord Annaly, Sir William Eden, Lord Henry Vane   *Front row*: Lord Castlereagh (left), Lady Helen Stewart (right).
Tempest.

Group outside Mountstewart *c*1890.
Back row: Lady Helen Stewart (left), Lord Castlereagh (4th
from left), N. W. Apperley (2nd from right), Theresa (right).
Front row: Lord Ormonde (2nd from left), 6th Marquess
(3rd from left) and A. J. Balfour next to him.
Photograph by Reginald.

Informal tea-party on the south-west terrace at Wynyard. 6th Marquess (left), Lady Helen Stewart (at head of table), Fräulein Sturmfels, Lord Castlereagh and Reginald behind him. Photograph by Theresa.

Group posed probably after a review of the local militia. *Front row*: Lord Herbert Vane Tempest (left), Lady Helen *Back row*: Lord Castlereagh (left), Adolphus Vane Tempest Stewart, 6th Marquess, Lord Henry Vane Tempest (right). next to him. Photograph by Reginald or Theresa.

Carriages drawn up outside Wynyard. The 6th Marquess hold-
ing the reins and whip on the first carriage, his brother Lord
Henry Vane Tempest standing just below him.
Photograph by Reginald *c*1890.

Ring-a-ring-of-roses (or so it would seem) in the grounds of
Mountstewart *c*1890. Photograph by Reginald or Theresa.

Group outside Wynyard *c*1890. Lord Herbert Vane Tempest
(2nd from left) and his brother Henry next to him. Lord
Londonderry is on the right with the Hon. James Lowther
beside him.

Cricket group at Wynyard. 6th Marquess standing at left, leaning on his stick, Theresa (3rd from left), stick in hand, Fräulein Sturmfels and Lord Castlereagh standing at the back (3rd and 5th from back).

Group taken during a shooting party.
Back row: The Hon. James Lowther (left), Viscount Coke (3rd from left), Lord Henry Vane Tempest (5th from right), Viscount Chaplin next to him, Lord Ormonde and N. W. Apperley on extreme right.
Front row: Lord Londonderry (left), Lady Randolph Churchill (next to him), Viscountess Coke (2nd from right). Photograph by Reginald or Theresa c1890.

Group at the foot of the steps to the broad walk at Wynyard.
Back row: The Hon. Harry West and Lady Helen Stewart (left and 2nd left), Lady Aline Allendale (right). *Centre*: Lord Castlereagh (left), 6th Marquess in centre. *Front row*: Lord Herbert Vane Tempest with stick. Photograph by Reginald or Theresa *c*1890.

Large group photographed at Mountstewart during the time the 6th Marquess was Lord Lieutenant of Ireland.

Back row, left to right: N. W. Apperley, Col. the Hon. Montague, Lord Coke, Lord Herbert Vane Tempest, Sir Henry Vane Tempest, Sir Henry Caltroft, Henry Chaplin, the Princess of Wales, the Hon. J. Lowther, the Prince of Wales, Lord Londonderry, Duke of Montrose, Lady Suffield, M. de Falbe, Duke of Clarence, Count Herbert Bismarck.

Front row: Col. Stanley Clark, Lord Cadogan, Duchess of Manchester, Duchess of Montrose, Lady Londonderry, Lady Dudley, Lady Coke, Lady Cadogan, Lady Randolph Churchill.

Group taken in the conservatory at Wynyard: Lord Lurgan is on the right at the back, with Lady Helen Stewart on his left. 6th Marquess on chair with unknown lady on his knee; A. J. Balfour on ground. Photograph by Reginald or Theresa *c*1890.

Group taken at Wynyard.
Back row: The Hon. James Lowther (3rd from left), Lord
Ormonde (4th from right), Christopher Sykes next to him.
Front row: Theresa (4th from left), 6th Marquess (3rd from
right), Lord Annaly next to him. Photograph by Reginald
*c*1890.

Formal photograph taken during the 6th Marquess's Lord Lieutenancy in Ireland. HRH Prince Albert Victor (later the ill-fated Duke of Clarence) is on Lord Londonderry's right, and Prince George (later King George V) is on his left.

Left:
The Londonderry Locomotive Engine in all its glory. The Londonderry Railway, running from Seaham to Sunderland, carried both passengers and goods. It was constructed by the 3rd Marquess and was a private family property until 1900. This engine may well have been driven by Reginald, who took the photograph.

Above:
Photograph of the drawing-room at Mountstewart. The picture on the left is of Charles Stewart, 3rd Marquess. Photograph by Reginald or Theresa *c*1890.

The old library at Wynyard, at the turn of the century. It is now
bare and unfurnished, but the beautiful book-cases remain.
Photograph by Reginald or Theresa.

Lady Londonderry's boudoir at Wynyard,
still in use today.

One of several follies at Wynyard. Photographed in the 1890s
by Reginald or Theresa.

Steps and interior of the Temple of the Three Graces. Signs of erosion can already be seen at the base of the columns, a process which continues unabating. The statues too are no longer as comely as they appear in the photograph; that on the right has disappeared altogether. Photographed in the 1890s by Reginald or Theresa.

View of the lake at Wynyard on a gloomy day. Photographed
by Reginald or Theresa *c*1890.

The Lion Bridge at Wynyard.
Photographed by Reginald or Theresa *c*1890.

The south-west face of Wynyard and the magnificent swing bridge which linked both sides of the valley near the house. The bridge was neglected between the wars and fell down in the early 1950s.

The south-west face of Wynyard from further back in the
valley. Photograph by Reginald or Theresa *c*1890.

View of the Italian Garden. In the background are the Ratisbon
gates of wrought iron which bear the date 1864 and are said to
have come from the cathedral at Ratisbon. They were brought
to Wynyard by Frances Anne, wife of the 3rd Marquess.
Photograph taken c1890 by Theresa.

A view of Strangford Loch near Mountstewart. Photograph
by Theresa *c*1890.

The Temple of the Four Winds at Mountstewart. While making the Grand Tour as a young man, the 1st Marquess came into contact with one James Stewart who was much interested in Greek antiquities. Stewart showed the Marquess a series of Grecian designs, one of which was of a famous temple in Athens called 'The Temple of the Winds'. Evidently the design was to the Marquess's liking, for shortly afterwards this striking octagonal garden-house was built.